IMAGES
of America

DOLLE'S
CANDYLAND, INC.

IMAGES
of America

DOLLE'S CANDYLAND, INC.

Anna Dolle Bushnell

ARCADIA
PUBLISHING

Published by Arcadia Publishing
Charleston, South Carolina

Library of Congress Control Number: 2020932417

For all general information, please contact Arcadia Publishing:
Telephone 843-853-2070
Fax 843-853-0044
E-mail sales@arcadiapublishing.com
For customer service and orders:
Toll-Free 1-888-313-2665

Visit us on the Internet at www.arcadiapublishing.com

*This book is dedicated to all of those touched by Dolle's Candyland.
A multigenerational business like Dolle's does not exist without
its family of loving staff, its tried and true customers, and the
communities that support it. We thank each and every one of our
longtime fans and hope that you enjoy a look into our past.*

CONTENTS

ACKNOWLEDGMENTS

Infinite thanks go out to my family for supporting this project. Its undertaking has opened doors to the past, much of which was unknown to me. My parents, Rudolph Dolle Jr. and Pamela Winters Dolle, have been wonderful family historians; they traveled near and far and spent countless hours researching our family. I am beyond honored to put a bit of their hard work into book form.

To my cousins Debi Thompson Cook, Marley Gunby, and Mary Dean Rouchard, thank you for your input and your photographs of a world of which I was not yet a part. Our family, and the business that they so loved, is certainly colorful, and it has been very entertaining to learn that we all get our traits honestly, from ancestors with such interesting lives.

Many thanks as well to Tom Ibach and Signe Holmgren-Murray for teaching me about a business very much like my own yet unique in its own special ways. I appreciate your stories and love the photographs you provided for this book. I am proud that the Dolle's of Rehoboth Beach still follows the same business practices and conveys the love that Dolle's of Ocean City strives for.

Special thanks must go out to Katelyn Jenkins and Caroline Anderson at Arcadia Publishing. Truth be told, this book began before I was formally approached to write it. I had organized photographs and begun collecting stories with no real direction. After a prayer or two, an email was received that Arcadia was interested in publishing a book on Dolle's. And now, here we are!

Endless thanks go out to my family members, deceased or still living, who thought it important to take so many pictures, and to those who kept those pictures safe. The collections are vast and it is a blessing that we have so much to share. Photographs for which no credit is given are from the private collection of the Dolle family.

INTRODUCTION

Since 1910, visitors and locals alike have enjoyed the sweet treats lovingly made by Dolle's (pronounced Doll-Eez) Candyland. With several other locations throughout its history, the original locations in Ocean City, Maryland, and Rehoboth Beach, Delaware, have remained staples of the landscape and culture of these popular Delmarva resorts.

Behind these storefronts lies a rich history of days gone by and a very positive outlook on the two companies' future success. Interwoven with the Dolle's history are the histories of other very well-known establishments, some long gone and some with very interesting outcomes and influences on Dolle's.

It is unlikely that anyone who has ever been to either Ocean City or Rehoboth Beach has not seen the iconic Dolle's signs in prime positions on the boardwalks of each beach town. The locations remain true to their roots, with family members continuing the tradition of making candy at the beach. The smell of caramel popcorn, freshly-made salt water taffy, and other beach treats have been emanating from these businesses for over a century, evoking an old-fashioned goodness unique to the shore.

Candy stores have been a mainstay on the streets of America's biggest cities and smallest towns for over a century. What sets Dolle's apart from other traditional candy shops is its history and its unique product offerings. In a world where American-made candies are becoming nothing but memories, salt water taffy, caramel popcorn, and other confections made by Dolle's remain relevant and popular. These products, packaged neatly in souvenir boxes, enable visitors to bring a taste of the beach back home.

Take a tour back in time with Dolle's as your looking glass. Look back to when the boardwalks of Rehoboth Beach and Ocean City were frequented by folks who traveled by train to the growing seaside resorts. See how the crowds and customer base grew because of the building of roads and bridges. View how stands and simple structures that were once built directly on the sand were replaced with sturdy foundations and walls to withstand hurricane winds. Learn when machinery was incorporated, starting with the first simple crank machine that replaced the need to hand pull, cut, and wrap each and every piece of taffy. Watch the business unfold over 110 years, and enjoy our history throughout these pages.

Our past is honored each and every day that we put on a white apron and begin the process of making candy and opening our doors for business. Sore backs from heavy lifting, burned skin, callused hands, exhausted minds, and tired bodies make up much of the day-to-day in family candy businesses. However, the opportunities to serve our customers, who often return year after year, generation after generation, as well as the ability to walk in our ancestors' footsteps, make the physical and mental challenges of candy making and business ownership an honor. We continue the long-standing tradition of candy making at Dolle's Candyland with an eye on the future and a respect for our past.

One

THE BEGINNINGS
OF A BUSINESS

In 1906, Rudolph William Dolle, aged 13, and his father, Rudolph Dolle, visited Ocean City, Maryland, on the invitation of Daniel Trimper of Trimper's Amusements. The purpose of the Dolles' trip was to find a location for their family-built carousel in the up-and-coming beach resort. This photograph was taken at the Ocean City Pier building on that scouting trip.

This postcard, dated 1911, shows a clear view of the Ocean City Pier building with Dolle's Candyland directly across the boardwalk on the corner of Wicomico Street. Ice-cream cones, salt water taffy, and honey-coated popcorn were the products sold at the stand. Called "the candy stand," it consisted of low serving counters with clear views of the candy manufacturing. Its construction was simple, built on a few rudimentary pilings under a thin flat roof. Directly behind the stand was the carousel, or merry-go-round, that the family operated.

Many Attractions

In Front of Pier

For guests and visitors to this delightful Beach, including the wonderful and enchanting

Merry=Go-Rounds

which has furnished much pleasure to the people. The Virginia Salt Water Taffy and Pop-Corn made on the the beach, once tasted, ever sought after.

DOLLE'S

The Popular Place. Opposite The Pier.

Joseph Schaefer's Bakery

And ICE CREAM PARLOR

FINEST ON THE PENINSULA

All kinds of Ice Cream, Bread, Pies and Cakes. Everything is First-class. Quality and refreshment in each plate and package. Baltimore Avenue, opposite Atlantic Hotel.

Joseph Schaefer,

Ocean City, Md.

This advertisement from 1911 boasts Dolle's as a true Ocean City attraction, complete with a merry-go-round and "Virginia Salt Water Taffy." After the Dolles purchased the property for their carousel, a man by the name of Greene offered his candy business to the family. They gladly purchased the business with the understanding that Greene would teach the Dolle children how to make the confections he had been making on the property. The family took to the business immediately and enjoyed making candy in addition to operating the carousel.

A heavy snowfall from a winter storm in 1914 proved too much for the simply built candy stand. The roof collapsed, forcing the Dolle family to rebuild. The building to the back of the demolished Dolle's is believed to have been a boardinghouse. To the right, in the background, is the famous Atlantic Hotel, built in 1875.

At center left, a small portion of the top of the Dolle's merry-go-round can be seen. It is not known if the stand collapse caused any damage to the carousel. To the right, just above the boardwalk, a sign for "Jersey Caramels" shows the front of the damaged counters.

Vashti Dennis of Hebron, Maryland, wed Rudolph "Rudy" Dolle in 1915. Both of their families committed to operating Dolle's Candyland. During the summers, the Dolles would live in Salisbury, Maryland, and in the winters in the neighborhood of Westport in Baltimore, Maryland. For some time, the Dolle family continued operating amusements in Baltimore's Druid Hill, Patterson, Carroll and Clifton Parks.

Frederick "Fred" Dolle, one of the three Dolle brothers, served in the military during the infancy of Dolle's beginning in 1917, when he was ordered to train at Fort Meade. During World War I, Corporal Dolle fought in battles in France, where he was injured from mustard gas.

After the collapse of the first candy stand, another simple building was constructed around 1919. Signage advertised sending salt water taffy via parcel post. Inside, salt water taffy is being pulled on a machine right behind the employee with his hand on his neck. At far right, a tiny onlooker, Evelyn Dolle at around three years old, peers in at her parents, Rudolph and Vashti Dolle. The sign maker had not completed painting the R and N in "Pop Corn" on the outside wall below the sign before this photograph was taken.

A rather dapper group enjoys the day on the boardwalk. The Dolle's popcorn sign was completed, and the interior of the stand was easy to see, along with a candy scale, shelving, and candy jars. Maggie Dennis, Vashti Dolle's sister, is the woman at right. The identities of the other people are unknown.

Dolle's Candyland became quite the popular place rather quickly. Display cases showed off crunchy caramel popcorn and chewy salt water taffy, while large jars were filled with mints and caramels—all right at eye level of young visitors. The flag banners were a favorite of Rudolph Dolle, who loved decorating for the Fourth of July, which was also his birthday.

Rudolph Dolle and his sister-in-law Francis "Fannie" Dolle pose in front of Dolle's on the corner of Wicomico Street and the boardwalk. At the time, the majority of the Dolle family and the Dennis family worked together at Dolle's.

Vashti Dolle stands with her mother-in-law, Amelia Hyle Dolle. Amelia, a New York City native, moved with her family (and their carousel) to Baltimore and later to Ocean City to operate the amusement ride. Both the Hyle and Dolle families, immigrants from Germany, were in the wood-carving trade. The Dolle family was related to and worked with Charles Looff, a famous carousel carver at the time. It is believed that the carousel that the Dolle family moved to Ocean City was built by Looff.

From left to right, Rudolph Dolle, Evelyn Dolle, and Ella Dennis (Vashti's sister) enjoy the boardwalk of Ocean City around 1920. In the background is the original Ocean City Pier building.

Fred Dolle, younger brother of Rudolph Dolle, poses on the beach with the original Ocean City Pier building in the background. The low roof of Dolle's can be seen on the left, as this photograph was taken on the south side of the pier building, facing north. The sign on the left side of the pier building reads "Ruth's Extra." This is where the famous Thrasher's French Fries stands today.

In 1922, Phillip "Phil" Dolle (far left) enjoys a crab feast with friends on the pier of Ocean City. Complete with beer and bare feet, they enjoyed a little downtime from the labor-intensive job of candy making.

Amanda Dennis, Vashti Dennis Dolle's mother, enjoys picking crabs with her son-in-law Rudolph Dolle on the Ocean City pier. The pier building was the center of town, so to speak, of Ocean City. It provided a place for shops and restaurants, a ballroom for dancing, and an extended fishing pier. It also protected buildings such as Dolle's against harsh winds and the elements. However, it was no match for a fire that swept through downtown Ocean City in 1925.

At around seven years old, Evelyn Dolle poses on the corner of Wicomico Street and the boardwalk. Behind her is the original Atlantic Hotel and signs advertising Showell's Baths and Pool as well as a sign for a local tailor offering hat cleaning. (Courtesy of Debi Thompson Cook.)

Rudolph and Vashti Dolle are seen in this photograph taken at Dolle's on Wicomico Street. According to Vashti's family, she was a very talented seamstress, hosting popular sewing parties at the couple's home in Salisbury.

Two

ANOTHER START

Amelia Hyle Dolle looks at the camera from behind the counter at Dolle's as her son mixes popcorn in a glass case. A woman walks away from the stand with a box of taffy in her arms and what appears to be a piece of candy in her hands. This is one of the last pictures of the stand before disaster struck.

On December 29, 1925, a fire started at a power plant on the corner of Somerset Street and Baltimore Avenue, just one block away from Dolle's. Three blocks of the downtown area including Dolle's, the pier building, and the Atlantic Hotel were completely destroyed. In this photograph, the remains that resemble the skeletal structure of an umbrella at far left are all that was left of the frame of the carousel. Unfortunately, the Ocean City Pier building, known to help shield the boardwalk from high winds and destructive surf, was no help in a fire. Fortunately, the business owners knew the benefits of continuing, and most, including the pier and the Atlantic Hotel, were rebuilt. (Courtesy of the Ocean City Life-Saving Station Museum, Ocean City, Maryland.)

From left to right, Vashti, Evelyn, and Rudolph Dolle pose on the boardwalk. Behind them is the new pier building under construction after the fire. (Courtesy of Debi Thompson Cook.)

After the fire of 1925, a new Dolle's building was erected. This photograph, taken around 1926, shows a second story, where apartments were built for the Dolle family and other tenants. This new and improved version of "the candy stand" still offered views of the caramel popcorn and salt water taffy manufacturing inside.

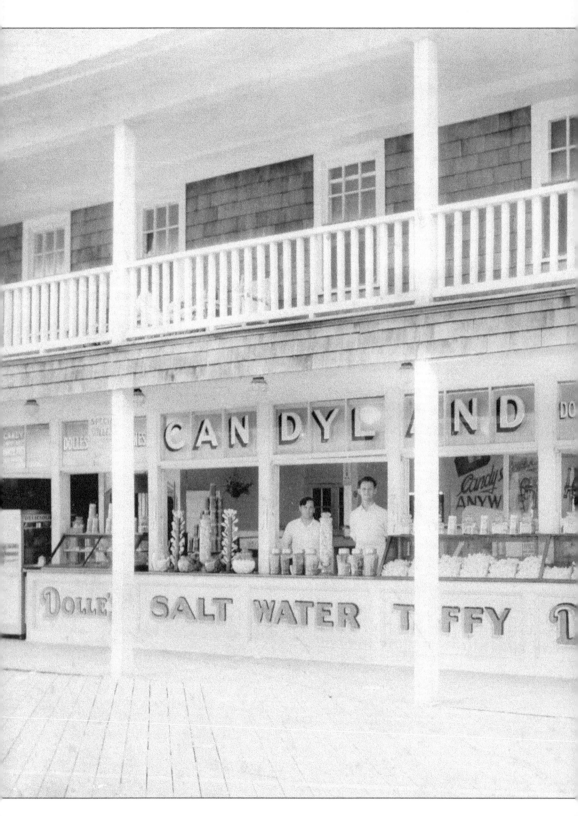

A beautiful storefront was something to be proud of for the Dennis and Dolle families. From left to right behind the counter are Rudolph Dolle, tall Michael Ward (brother-in-law of Vashti), Hazel Dolle (first wife of Fred Dolle), Vashti Dolle, and unidentified. Signs around the store advertise a special on salt water taffy: 35¢ per pound or three pounds for $1. Lollipops, salt water taffy, and a modern popping corn machine are all featured in the front displays. At the time, salt water taffy was manufactured in several different flavors, including vanilla, chocolate, strawberry, lime, lemon, orange, molasses, black walnut, anise, peppermint, and spearmint. It was cooked to a high temperature, producing a rather hard (but still chewy) candy that could withstand heat and humidity. (Courtesy of Debi Thompson Cook.)

Dolle's famous salt water taffy was packaged in one pound and one-half pound boxes as well as being offered by the piece. The boxes consisted of a rigid cardboard bottom and a rigid cardboard top wrapped in printed paper (also known as a "lid wrap"). The design of these boxes was borrowed from oyster houses of the late 1800s. One pound of salt water taffy fit perfectly in the same boxes for one pound of oysters. Artwork of beachgoers and ocean waves adorned the sides and top of the box on the lid wrap. Beachgoers were also illustrated on the top and side panels of the boxes. Dolle's took hold of the salt water taffy market, claiming theirs to be the "original" salt water taffy of Ocean City. This box is from the mid-1920s.

During this time, Dolle's had several locations throughout Maryland, including Salisbury, Baltimore, Public Landing, and additional stands in Ocean City. This particular Dolle's was on First Street and the boardwalk. The Dolle family had holdings in the Essex Hotel, which had retail locations on the boardwalk. From left to right are Phillip Dolle, Hazel Dolle, Fannie Dolle (in front), Fred Dolle, and Lloyd Dennis (Vashti's brother). (Courtesy of Debi Thompson Cook.)

From left to right, Evelyn Dolle, Vashti Dolle, and Margaret Kroeger sit on a bench on the boardwalk in Ocean City. Next to them are a soda fountain and a business selling postcards.

Salt water taffy production was quite labor intensive in the early days. After pulling the candy, it had to be hand rolled into a log, cut by hand, and then wrapped in waxed paper. Pictured is the first crank cutting machine, made by Thomas Mills of Philadelphia, Pennsylvania. Candy was formed by hand into a thin rope and then fed into this machine. As the machine was cranked, the candy would be cut into pieces, which still had to be wrapped individually by hand.

In the mid-1930s, Dolle's purchased its first cutting and wrapping machine, which eliminated the tedious practice of slowly cutting and manually wrapping each individual piece of taffy. Pictured is the cover of the manual for the second machine purchased by Dolle's. Notes were written on the cover over the years, including a telephone number. The manual was singed in a fire decades later.

Three

REACHING NEW SHORES

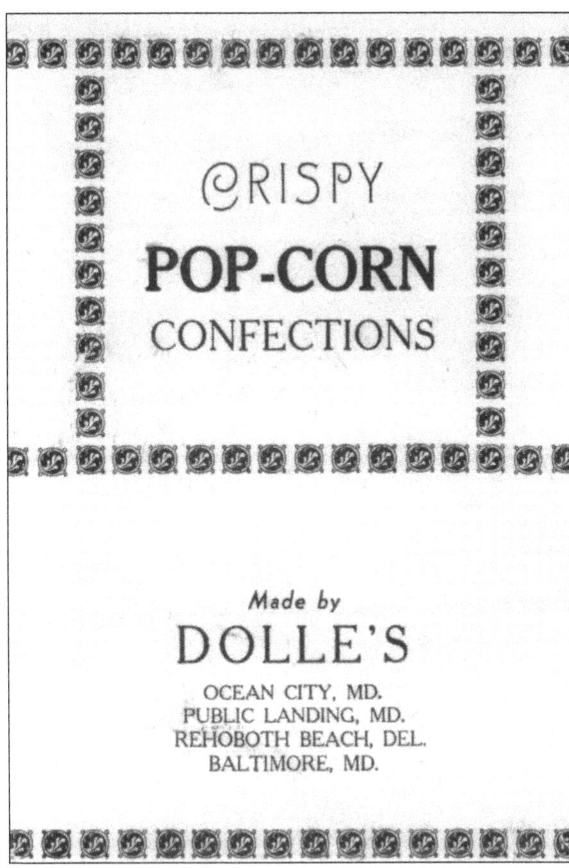

This popcorn box from the late 1920s shows all of Dolle's locations at the time: Ocean City, Public Landing (Snow Hill), Baltimore, and Rehoboth Beach. The square graphics on the box would soon be replaced with the iconic black diamond border that continues to be used on the popcorn packaging to this day.

CRISPY

POP-CORN

CONFECTIONS

Made by

DOLLE'S

OCEAN CITY, MD.
PUBLIC LANDING, MD.
REHOBOTH BEACH, DEL.
BALTIMORE, MD.

Around 1913, Rudolph Dolle met Thomas Pachides, a candy maker in Philadelphia. Candy stores were common, especially in major cities such as Philadelphia, as immigrants brought their old-world expertise to the United States. Pachides, a Greek immigrant, learned to be a candy maker and operated an ice cream parlor and soda fountain of his own in the city. He began coming to Ocean City in the summers to work for the Dolle family. After working together for a short while teaching Dolle the craft of candy making, Pachides moved to Salisbury with his wife, Theo, and three young daughters, Constance, Alexandra, and Helen. There, he operated a wholesale candy company. Later, Dolle and Pachides began working on plans intending to expand the Dolle's business. In 1926, the two families opened a Dolle's Candyland in Rehoboth Beach. A year later, they purchased the YMCA building in Rehoboth Beach for $10,000. Their new location was on the northeast corner of Rehoboth Avenue and the Rehoboth Beach boardwalk, exactly where it remains today. (Courtesy of Thomas Ibach.)

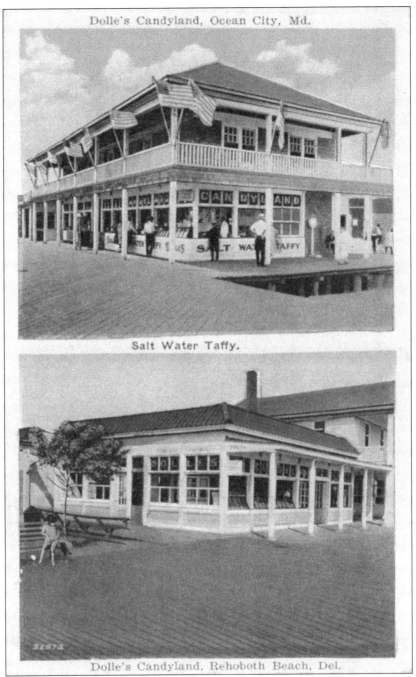

Dolle's Candyland, Ocean City, Md.

Salt Water Taffy.

Dolle's Candyland, Rehoboth Beach, Del.

This postcard shows the two main Dolle's locations—Ocean City and Rehoboth Beach. In Rehoboth Beach, the Dolle's building included an arcade on the north end and a bowling alley in the back. The bowling alley had several lanes where duck pin bowling was played. Pin setters worked quickly to reset the pins and often signed the stations where they worked. Their signatures and flooring from the bowling alley remain behind the current Dolle's building. According to Pachides's grandson Thomas Ibach, his grandfather shut the bowling alley down abruptly in the 1930s after a priest tried to unionize the pin setters. (Courtesy of Thomas Ibach.)

Thomas Pachides stands at center in this photograph in front of Dolle's (from a southwestern vantage point). His wife, Theo, is seen walking at left. The man in the swimsuit and sweater is unidentified. Pachides was well known as a wonderful candy maker with a dedication to the trade. He loved making candy while his wife took the helm running the business. (Courtesy of Signe Holmgren-Murray.)

Thomas Pachides was an avid fisherman and caught this sizable fish from the surf. He was very generous and would often give his catches to friends and neighbors. There is a story that he nearly put the fish markets of Rehoboth Beach out of business due to his generosity and was kindly asked to refrain from giving away fish. (Courtesy of Signe Holmgren-Murray.)

Salt water taffy was and still is considered a perfect souvenir for beachgoers. This box features an image of the Cape Henlopen Lighthouse in Lewes, Delaware, along with seagulls and waves, as well as a new Dolle's logo, complete with a tail with the words "salt water taffy" inside. On the sides of the box were illustrations of both the Ocean City and Rehoboth Beach stores. These regional images in addition to the delicious candy inside made for a perfect memento from the beach.

CAPE HENLOPEN LIGHTHOUSE, REHOBOTH BEACH, DEL.

This postcard of the Cape Henlopen Lighthouse may have been the inspiration for the artwork on the Dolle's salt water taffy box. The image is still used today by the Dolle's in Rehoboth Beach. A home that Rudolph Dolle built in the 1940s had a chimney and fireplace constructed with some of the original granite stones collected from the beach after this lighthouse collapsed in 1926.

Four

DOLLE'S EARLY DAYS

Candies that are not subject to heat or humidity have been the staples of Dolle's. Since air-conditioning was not available, candy that could withstand the elements was key. Salt water taffy, caramel popcorn, fudge, and caramels were the first candies produced and served to visitors. Beginning in the 1930s, more modern candy and popcorn-making equipment had been developed, such as this popcorn case and popper, which helped in keeping up with demand from the growing crowds.

In the early 1930s, Vashti's brother Lloyd Dennis Sr. (left) and an unidentified employee take a break from candy making. White pants, white shirts, and an apron were the standard candy-makers' uniforms. They kept staff cool and protected them from the rigors of candy making.

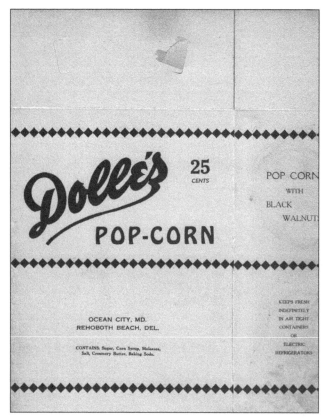

Popcorn packaging at Dolle's has remained consistent throughout its history. Simple cardboard boxes continue to be used. The diamond border design seen here was used in Dolle's newspaper advertisements, appearing in local papers beginning in 1915. Throughout the company's history, caramel popcorn varieties always included plain caramel, but starting in the 1920s, caramel corn with black walnuts, and caramel popcorn with peanuts and "cocoanut" were sold, as seen on the side panel of this box. The box measures approximately 12 by 6 by 2 inches—a lot of popcorn for 25¢.

As seen on many of the signs at Dolle's, customers were encouraged to buy candy and have it shipped. Pictured here is a receipt for a mail order. When a customer wished to send a package from Dolle's, they were given a mailing label to fill out. After they filled out the label, they were given the tear-off section as a receipt. Note that no figures are given, only the date and type of candy, along with an invoice number. What is even more curious is that the actual label that the customer filled out was glued directly to the parcel it was shipped on. If a customer wanted to find the whereabouts of their package, the information (the invoice number matching their receipt) would only be on the package that was shipped. This very simple documentation evolved throughout the years to be more efficient. With the age of technology, tracking packages became as simple as clicking a few buttons.

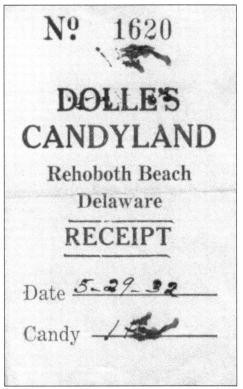

Vashti Dolle poses facing south on the boardwalk in front of the Dolle's on Wicomico Street. Behind her is the new pier building to the right, with the Alaska Stand at left. The Alaska Stand, owned by the Givarz family, sold Alaskas, which were chocolate-coated vanilla ice cream blocks on a stick. Through the years, they added frozen bananas, fruit juices, and burgers and French fries. The Givarz family ran this location until 1991, when it was sold and the name changed.

Fred Dolle appears at left in his white uniform and looks to be talking to Thomas Pachides (sitting on the bench) in this photograph of the Dolle's of Rehoboth Beach. In the Dolle's building, the second awning to the left advertises Alaskas and Crane's Ice Cream (a predominantly Philadelphia-

made ice cream at the time). It is quite possible that the neighboring Givarz family from Ocean City may have rented this space for their business in Rehoboth Beach. (Courtesy of Thomas Ibach.)

In addition to the candy business, the Dolles owned and operated a restaurant, located directly behind the candy stand in Ocean City (far right). It was built with the kitchen in the back and two apartments on the second floor. The Gunther's Beer sign on the roof advertised beer sales at both the candy stand and at the restaurant. During World War II, Dolle's Candyland was affected by strict sugar rationing. Family members would travel to Baltimore to attain their allotments of sugar. Dolle's set a sales limit of three pounds of taffy per customer. The low supply and the sales cap meant that most customers bought the maximum allowed. After all the candy was sold, Dolle's simply closed its rolling doors.

The restaurant employed several family members, and Amelia Hyle Dolle made the desserts. On the eastern corner of the building was a barbershop rented by Press Davis, a well-known barber in Ocean City. A man named Sy Jarvis worked in the restaurant. When it closed a few years later, Jarvis purchased the equipment and used it in his new restaurant, City Lunch, on the corner of Baltimore Avenue and Wicomico Street.

Around the time Dolle's Restaurant began, Evelyn Dolle married Harper Dean. She gave birth on August 19, 1936, to Mary Dean, Rudolph and Vashti's first grandchild.

Next to the restaurant building on Wicomico Street, Dolle's acquired several additional small structures. Included were the two buildings featured in this photograph with the signs "Ice Cream" and "Rest Rooms." Rudolph Dolle had an agreement with the Town of Ocean City that the building at 9 Wicomico Street would remain public restrooms. It operated as such until the 1950s, when the town opened a public comfort station on the boardwalk at Worcester Street. After the restrooms were moved, the small building was renovated into the Sweet Pea Apartments. Shortly thereafter, the building housed a Mr. Donut and then a flower shop and was later used for storage. Later, it was turned into a salt water taffy factory. The cottage housing the ice cream shop was converted into a peanut shack, and later a game of skill was set up inside.

In 1938, Amelia Heyl Dolle passed away. Rudolph Dolle then purchased the entirety of shares of the business from his brothers and sisters. Secondary shops closed, while the original Dolle's on Wicomico Street and the Dolle's of Rehoboth Beach thrived. Philip, Rudolph, and Fred Dolle are pictured here in front of the candy stand in the late 1930s.

Cousins Mary Dean and Lloyd Dennis Jr. share some fun with a tricycle on the boardwalk. The signs in the candy stand offer walnut, peanut, and coconut popcorn. The counters had been replaced with counters on casters, which made it easy to configure the display areas as needed.

Rudolph Dolle takes a spin on a tricycle of his own. The photograph was taken in front of Ralph's, a luncheonette on the south end of the Dolle's building. The enameled lollipop-style Toledo scale at right was a fixture on the outside of Dolle's until the 1970s. It is still owned by the Dolle family, but is now stored inside.

Mary Dean is pictured with her favorite doll on the benches on Wicomico Street. Behind her are signs for Dolle's popcorn and the stairs leading up to the apartments where she lived.

Lloyd Dennis Jr. has his cart filled with wrapped boxes of candy ready to go to the post office. Primarily salt water taffy was shipped from Dolle's as it held up well in the mail. Salt water taffy was seen as a perfect gift, and one that the purchaser did not need to carry back home. In nearly every photograph of a Dolle's business, there is sign advertising the ability to ship candy directly from the stands.

In 1934, an ice cream shop in the pier building, directly across from Dolle's, was owned and operated by Gladys and Bernie Thrush. Known as Bernie's Boardwalk Dairyland, the business thrived until Gladys divorced Bernie and married Pete Dumser. The business was then renamed Dumsers, and the couple operated it in a new location, right across the pier, in the Dolle's building. The Dumsers lived in one of the apartments above Dolle's Candyland, next to members of the Dolle family. Pete Dumser was a well-known musician and played the organ in his ice cream shop to attract customers.

The 1940s were a heyday for Dolle's. Record sales were made during this time thanks to improvements to roadways and, in Ocean City, the opening of the Route 50 bridge, which funneled traffic directly to the lower end of town. The growing popularity of the two resort towns meant more visitors.

Dolle business ventures expanded into the beginnings of the food truck market. The Candyland Kandy Kar traveled to resort areas in Maryland and Delaware selling "Karmel Korn" and salt water taffy from its doors. It is not known what happened to the Kandy Kar.

A party was held inside Dolle's Restaurant celebrating Mary Dean's sixth birthday on August 19, 1942. The guest list consisted of classmates, friends, and family. From left to right in the first row are two unidentified, John Dennis, Connie Dennis, Mitch Marianna, Bernice Anne Thrush (the daughter of Gladys Thrush Dumser), and two unidentified. Among the others are Ida Dennis, Thelma Milian, Rudolph Dolle, Vashti Dolle, and Edith Roberts. (Courtesy of Debi Thompson Cook.)

This paper placemat from Dolle's Restaurant shows a map of the Delmarva Peninsula with three Dolle's Candyland businesses in Ocean City, Rehoboth Beach, and Bethany Beach, Delaware. (Courtesy of Patti Soriano.)

W.B. MANGELS, PRESIDENT
W.H. MANGELS, TREASURER

CABLE ADDRESS "MANHERCO"
A.B.C. 5TH EDITION, IMP.
TELEPHONE, SOUTH 0049

FROM PINTS TO CARS

MANGELS, HEROLD CO., INC.

Importers and Refiners
SYRUPS AND MOLASSES

KEY HIGHWAY & BOYLE ST.
BALTIMORE, MD.

June 25, 19 45

M   Rudolph Dolle

OceanCity, Maryland

ALL CLAIMS MUST BE MADE WITHIN 7 DAYS AFTER RECEIPT OF GOODS.

3	bbl. Corn Syrup		
	762-67		
	766-67		
	744-65		
	2272-199-2073 @ 4.62	95	77
	Less 2%	1	92
		93	85

Pictured is a receipt for corn syrup from Mangels Herold Company in Baltimore. It shows a sale of three barrels of corn syrup totalling 2,073 pounds and costing 4.62¢ per pound before a two percent discount. Corn syrup and sugar are the main ingredients in salt water taffy and caramel popcorn.

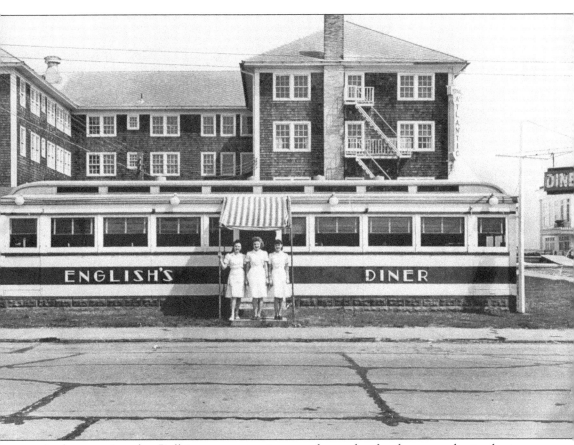

At the same time that Dolle's was experiencing growth, another family was conducting business one block north. Located between Wicomico and Somerset Streets on Baltimore Avenue, Carlton and Anna English opened English's Diner in 1940. Behind the diner stands the Atlantic Hotel. At far right, the pier building can be seen.

Carlton and Anna English of Salisbury pose in front of their diner. Carlton English and his brother James Hilton English opened several diners and restaurants on the Delmarva Peninsula. Specializing in Eastern Shore favorites such as chicken and (slippery) dumplings and fried chicken, which was made with a unique blend of spices producing a red-hued frying batter, English's Diner and their other restaurants were popular places to dine.

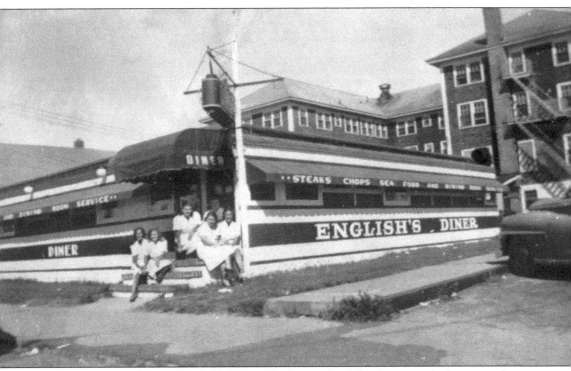

Waitresses pose in front of English's Diner. To the north of the diner stands the original post office building for Ocean City, located on the corner of Somerset Street and Baltimore Avenue. Behind the diner is the Atlantic Hotel.

Rudolph Dolle sits on the porch above Dolle's Candyland overlooking the boardwalk. Around this time, Dolle frequented English's Diner, where he became enamored with a waitress, Elaine, the daughter of Carlton and Anna English. At the time, Elaine was recently divorced from Raymond Ferry, a cook at the diner.

In December of 1946, Vashti Dolle fell extremely ill with heart complications. At the time, she and Rudolph Dolle were estranged. She passed away on January 19, 1947. Here, she is seen in front of the shop on First Street and the boardwalk.

In 1947, Rudolph Dolle built a home in Bethany Beach. Elaine English, along with her daughter Elaine Elsie Ferry, age seven at the time, moved to the home. On July 17, 1949, Elaine English gave birth to Rudolph W. Dolle Jr. Pictured are Elaine Ferry (nine years old) and her little brother Rudolph Dolle Jr.

Pictured in 1947 is the home built by Rudolph Dolle in Bethany Beach. The construction was typical of many of the homes built at that time. It had a cinderblock frame finished with white stucco, black shutters, and three-quarter-inch knotty pine panels on the interior. The Cape Henlopen Lighthouse granite stones used in the chimney can be seen here.

In the late 1940s, partners Rudolph Dolle and Tom Pachides purchased an additional plot of land, possibly to build another Dolle's Candyland, on the corner of Garfield Avenue and the boardwalk in Bethany Beach. A theater had been on the property but was washed away during a storm. The pilings of the theater remained, along with three small cottages, when the land was purchased. Pictured in downtown Bethany Beach are Rudolph Dolle holding young Rudolph Dolle Jr. while Elaine English looks on.

Five

THE 1950S

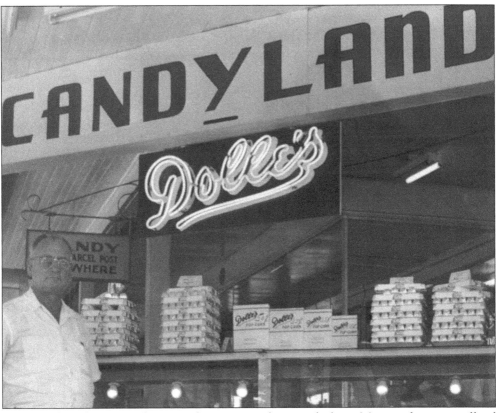

The 1950s brought new machinery and some unique business dealings. More products were offered as air-conditioning became available. Here, Rudolph Dolle stands in front of the popcorn display with a new blue neon "Dolle's" sign.

In 1953, Rudolph Dolle and Thomas Pachides purchased two Forgrove taffy cut and wrap machines at $6,000 each for both Dolle's locations. In this photograph, Lloyd Dennis is pictured at far right packing taffy, while employee Glen Balentine stands at left inspecting the candy as it exits the machine. Rudolph Dolle is shaping the taffy and feeding it into the new machine. After the taffy was stretched by hand to fit inside the machine, it was cut and then wrapped in cellophane at a speed of 400–500 pieces per minute. This particular machine cut "stick" or long-style salt water taffy. More developments and acquisitions like this machine increased productivity, which was necessary to keep up with demand. These machines are still in use today; however, at Dolle's in Ocean City, the machine was modified to use waxed paper while the Dolle's in Rehoboth Beach continues to use cellophane wrapping.

Pictured is salt water taffy that was cut and wrapped on the Rose Forgrove machine. The stripes on the taffy are to indicate the flavor. Contrary to what some believe, the flavor is not in the stripes; rather, the flavor is pulled throughout the entire batch of candy before it is cut and wrapped.

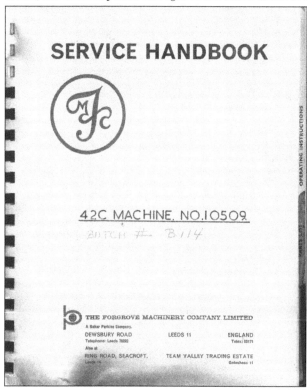

Pictured is the front of the manual for the Forgrove machine shown on the previous page. The specialized machine was built in England, and very few people at the time (or even now) are familiar with its inner workings. The manuals were priceless in that they were the first resource when the machines broke down. The operators often double as engineers, as time lost on production can be detrimental.

Evelyn Dean (left) and Mary Dean model chocolate bars with Rudolph Dolle. These particular chocolate bars were purchased by a fledgling company called World's Finest Chocolate, now a nationally known fundraising product made in Chicago. In this image, the chocolate bars, a rather precarious product to serve at the beach, are on display on the popcorn cases. Signs advertised their availability, but they were rarely out on display as seen here.

From left to right, Nellie Gibbs, Dollie Brittingham, Thelma Milian, Edith Roberts (Thelma Milian's mother), and Rudolph Dolle stand in front of the popcorn display cases. Nellie Gibbs began working for the Dolle family in 1922. Rudolph had a wonderful relationship with "Mrs. Gibbs," as she was always addressed. Her grandchildren and great grandchildren would later found and operate the Dough Roller restaurants in Ocean City.

TRY OUR
SALT WATER TAFFY

FUDGE – CARAMELS
AND CANDIES

Dolle's®

POP-CORN

KEEPS FRESH

INDEFINITELY

IN AIR TIGHT

CONTAINERS

OR

ELECTRIC

REFRIGERATORS

OCEAN CITY, MD. 21842
REHOBOTH BEACH, DEL. 19971

CONTAINS: POP CORN, SUGAR, CORN SYRUP,
SALT, EDIBLE OILS, CREAMERY BUTTER, BAKING
SODA. MAY ALSO CONTAIN MOLASSES.

QUALITY CANDY SINCE 1910

The smallest size box for caramel popcorn, containing approximately two servings, sold for 15¢ in the early 1950s. At the time, the boxes needed to be folded by hand. The job of putting the boxes together was often handled by the youngest family members. However, the tedious task was necessary in order to prepare for the busy rushes.

The salt water taffy boxes in the 1950s depicted the Cape Henlopen lighthouse as well as more detailed weights and measurements than in the past. The two shops shared the same box design, as it was cheaper to print larger quantities of the wrap for the lid.

In 1957, Rudolph Dolle sits on a bench on Wicomico Street with his granddaughter Mary Dean Thompson, daughter Evelyn Dolle Dean Adams, and great-granddaughter Debi Thompson. Behind them, cars are lined up on the street, signifying a busy day at the beach.

In the late 1950s, Thomas Pachides sits with grandson Thomas Ibach, granddaughter Signe (Holmgren) Murray, and wife Theo in their Rehoboth Beach home. Thomas Ibach is the son of Alexandra Pachides Ibach, and Signe Murray is the daughter of Helen Pachides Holmgren. (Courtesy of Signe Holmgren Murray.)

Behind the scenes on a busy day on the boardwalk, Evelyn Dolle serves popcorn out of the case at Dolle's in Ocean City. In order to keep up with the demand of large crowds, cooks would prepare caramel popcorn and store it in large tins (seen on the right). The prepared popcorn was mixed in with the popcorn that was constantly being made. This tactic was used quite frequently, as the small batches did not yield enough product to keep up with demand. Below, note the gladiolas on the counter. Live plants and flowers were often used as decoration in the building. Nellie Gibbs was known to be proud of her sweet potato plants that she nurtured within the candy stand. Her plants would grow to great lengths along the walls and ceiling of the stand. (Both, courtesy of Debi Thompson Cook.)

Fudge is a staple of Dolle's Candyland. Pictured is packaging used for fudge by both the Rehoboth Beach and Ocean City Dolle's shops. The packaging features design elements that match the salt water taffy boxes, including the Cape Henlopen Lighthouse and the standardized Dolle's logo. The print was in dark blue, not colorful like the taffy boxes.

Mellow Mint Sticks have been a mainstay of the product line at Dolle's. Similar to salt water taffy in that it is pulled (or aerated), its unique melt-in-your-mouth consistency and strong peppermint taste is what differentiates the mints from taffy. Originally formed into braids about eight inches long and stored in jars for display, these candies took on a new form with the purchase of the Forgrove "stick" machine.

In 1959, Rudolph Dolle built the Blue Surf Motel on the corner of the boardwalk and Garfield Avenue in Bethany Beach on the land he and Thomas Pachides had acquired. The oceanfront hotel was built by Harry Kellem, the son-in-law of Carlton and Anna English and brother-in-law to Elaine English Dolle. Carlton and Anna English were the first people to run the motel, while their daughter Elaine ran the small gift shop inside. On December 29, 1959, Tom Pachides and Rudolph Dolle exchanged shares in the businesses that they had purchased together. Dolle sold his shares of the Dolle's of Rehoboth Beach to Pachides, and Pachides sold his shares of the Blue Surf Motel in Bethany Beach to Dolle.

Six

THE 1960s

The 1960s proved to be a challenging decade for the Pachides and Dolle families. However, natural disasters, deaths, and other issues were overcome. Dolle's picked up the pieces, so to speak, and continued on.

Katherine Shapowal Roberg is pictured behind the popcorn counter of Dolle's in September 1961. Roberg, a Philadelphia native, began working for the Dolle family in Ocean City in 1955. She and her husband, Swain, lived in an apartment above the Dolle's Restaurant building.

In the early 1960s, Rudolph Dolle sits on a bench on Wicomico Street by Billy's Sub Shop, in the corner of the building that housed Dolle's Restaurant. His granddaughter Mary Dean Thompson started Billy's Sub Shop with her husband, Billy Thompson, in 1959. Dorrette and Dean Thompson, the Thompsons' children, are pictured playing in front of the shop.

On Ash Wednesday 1962, the shorelines of Delaware and Maryland were pummeled by a nor'easter that produced high winds and record-breaking flooding. Pictured at right is damage to the Blue Surf Motel. The aerial shot of the Blue Surf Motel and downtown Bethany Beach below shows the devastation. Just a few miles up the Delaware coast, Dolle's in Rehoboth Beach was in shambles. The 35-year-old building could not withstand the winds and tide. The entire building was in pieces in the surf. Photographs were lost, and the Pachides family did all they could to salvage any piece of their business. Friends and family held machine manuals above their heads through the wild surf in efforts to save them. The 3,500-pound taffy machine fell through the floor and into the water.

After the 1962 storm destroyed the entire building, Tom Pachides reconstructed the Dolle's building. According to his grandchildren Tom Ibach and Signe Holmgren Murray, their grandmother Theo absolutely loved the business, and her husband rebuilt it for her. Apartments were built on top of the store for the Pachides family. Impressively, the business was up and running by July. Shortly after the rebuild, the famous Dolle's sign was erected on the roof. The sign was originally constructed of plywood and painted bright red, becoming one of the most recognizable icons of the Rehoboth Beach skyline.

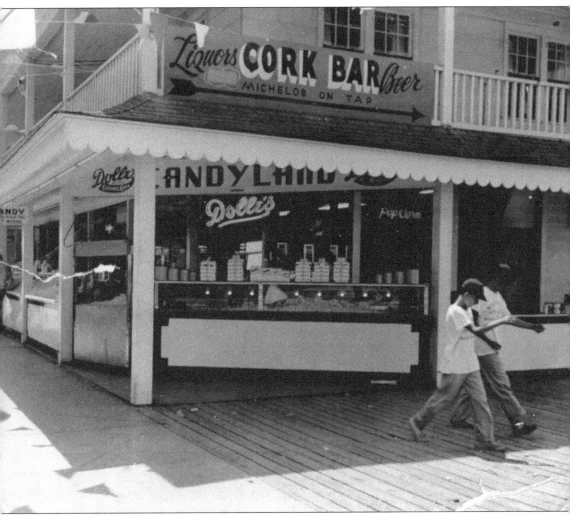

In 1962, another iconic Ocean City business was born, the Cork Bar. Housed in the former Dolle's Restaurant, the Cork Bar was started by Mitch Parker and later owned by Dan Freck. In 1964, John Mazko and Morris Wilkins took over. The Cork Bar has been known as the place for the coldest beer in town, with draught beer still poured into frozen glass mugs. In this photograph, a sign on the Dolle's building advertises the bar just steps off the boardwalk.

Rudolph Dolle Jr., known as "Bunky," began working at Dolle's at the age of 12. His first jobs included setting up the popcorn boxes and packing salt water taffy. At the time, salt water taffy was packed using a "ferris wheel," a unique piece of equipment built by Bunky's father. Employees would sit on either side of the spinning apparatus, which had salt water taffy stored in bins by individual flavors. The motorized wheel would move slowly as the employees picked taffy out of each bin and neatly placed it in rows in the boxes. Memories of the "ferris wheel" are vivid, as it was an attraction to watch. However, those working on the machine had to be extremely careful not to knock one of the filled taffy bins off the wheel, causing pounds of candy to fall to the floor. Bunky is pictured here in 1965 learning to operate the salt water taffy machine his father purchased in 1953. (Courtesy of Debi Thompson Cook.)

From left to right, Judy Shapowal, Katherine Roberg, Nellie Gibbs, and Linda Bunting (sister in law of Nellie Gibbs) are pictured here, with Bunky Dolle in the background. Katherine Roberg originally came to Ocean City to waitress and later moved on to a managerial position at Dolle's. Judy Shapowal is her niece.

In 1960, Evelyn Dolle Dean Adams Gunby (right) gave birth to Marley Gunby (center), Mary Dean Thompson's younger sister and 24 years her junior. They are pictured here with Elaine English Dolle at the Dolle home in Bethany Beach. Although the family had quite an interesting tree, the members on all sides, whether estranged, divorced, or otherwise, got along very well.

From left to right, Fred Dolle, Rudolph Dolle, Carrie Dolle Kaline, George Kaline, and Lloyd Kramer (Rudolph's lifelong friend) sit on the boardwalk benches on Wicomico Street. Amelia, the Dolles' other sister, is the only sibling missing from this picture. Behind them is a clear view of Billy's Subs and Elliott's Hardware. A sign for ice was directed at fishermen on Sinepuxent Bay, advertising the ice factory on Philadelphia Avenue. This photograph from September 1968 is the last image of the Dolle siblings together. In December, Rudolph Dolle passed away at the age of 75, shortly after his wife, Elaine English Dolle, died in 1967 at the age of 46.

Thomas Pachides is pictured in 1969 making salt water taffy in his new building in Rehoboth Beach. Here, he forms the taffy as it rolls on wooden rollers. The rollers help make the candy the correct size to fit into the machine, turning it from a large mass into a thin rope. The machine that the candy is going into cuts and wraps the "kiss" style of taffy, as seen below. (Both, courtesy of Signe Holmgren Murray.)

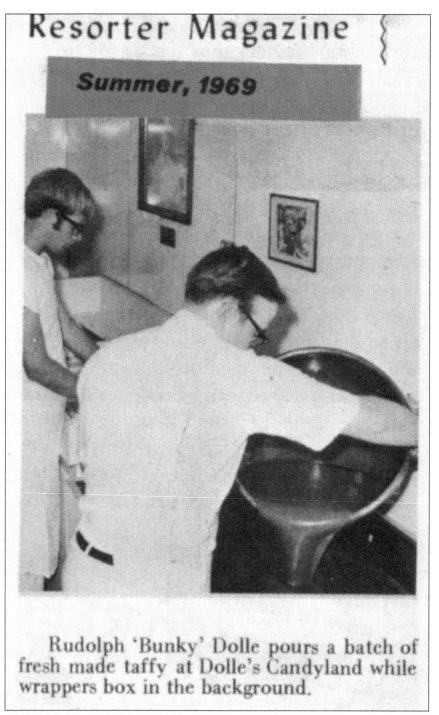

Resorter Magazine

Summer, 1969

Rudolph 'Bunky' Dolle pours a batch of fresh made taffy at Dolle's Candyland while wrappers box in the background.

Bunky Dolle (right) pours freshly cooked liquid salt water taffy onto a cooling table. The taffy was cooked in an open copper kettle, producing 25 pounds of candy. It was cooled on water-jacketed tables, then pulled. The aeration gives taffy its signature chewiness; this is also when flavors are added. After pulling, it is cut and wrapped on machines before it is packaged. Donald Timmons, childhood friend of Bunky, is at left.

In the late 1960s, Billy and Mary Thompson expanded their sub shop to include an outdoor patio. Here, the small cottage that was between the sub shop and 9 Wicomico Street was razed to make room for the patio. The cottage was originally a peanut shack and later housed a game of skill that required a player to knock down pins using a ball tied to a string hung from the ceiling. Apparently, news got out that the game was rigged. It was shut down after an intoxicated Marine lost over $600. Apparently, Rudolph Dolle was so upset that he immediately shut the game down and tore the building down. The apartments in the background were occupied by Evelyn Dolle, Rudolph Dolle, and Donald Timmons at various times. (Courtesy of Debi Thompson Cook.)

Billy's Sub Shop, along with many of the other local eateries, was supplied with fresh ingredients by farmers and local vendors. Here, Mary Dean Thompson haggles while Deanie Thompson picks out ears of corn from the back of a vendor's car on Wicomico Street. It was not uncommon to see the Thompson children running around the boardwalk while their parents worked. They all lived in apartments over Dolle's and have vivid memories of their childhood days at the beach. Debi, Deanie, and Dorrette, along with their Mancini cousins, enjoyed the beach but were known to get in a bit of trouble. Once, Deanie ventured into the attic of the apartments, only to fall through the living room ceiling of Pete and Gladys Dumser. (Courtesy of Debi Thompson Cook.)

The north facade of Dolle's shows a plethora of painted signs, including a large one for Billy's. Rudolph Dolle claimed that Billy's was so busy, it might be doing more business than Dolle's. Billy's eventually moved off Wicomico Street to larger locations in other areas of Ocean City.

Seven

THE 1970S

The 1970s proved to be another decade of change and hard work for the Dolle and Pachides families. The famous Dolle's sign in Delaware also needed a bit of extra attention when the large red D fell off. The entire sign was remade, this time with a more structurally sound material than painted plywood. The new sign was painted orange, with a paint that would resist weathering.

Evelyn Dolle Dean Adams Gunby is pictured next to a tall stack of salt water taffy boxes in the early 1970s. Before the 1970s, each box was gift wrapped in striped Dolle's-branded wrapping paper. After it was questioned why all the beautiful artwork on the boxes was being covered, Dolle's moved to wrapping each box in cellophane. The cellophane was folded around the boxes and then heat sealed on the ends with a hot pad. Each box was painstakingly wrapped by hand, and a special technique had to be learned by employees to avoid burning their fingertips. Evelyn was known to also heat breakfast pastries on the hot pads.

In 1971, Bunky Dolle enlisted in the Navy. While he was serving around the world, manager Katherine Roberg and Bunky's friend Donald Timmons ran the candy stand in Ocean City. Evelyn's health was beginning to fail, and at 22 years old, Bunky had to depend on Katherine and Donnie to keep the business running smoothly.

Bunky Dolle served in the Navy until 1977. During his leave, he would often come home to make candy, his true passion in life. Here, Bunky watches a candy thermometer as he cooks a batch of salt water taffy.

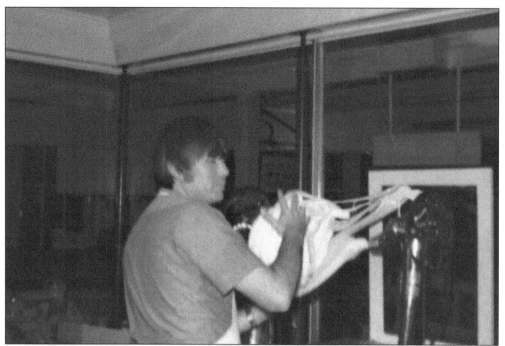

In his Navy shirt, Bunky Dolle pulls aerated salt water taffy off the pulling machine, which has four hooks that pull air into the candy. This machine dated to the 1920s and can be seen in many of the early pictures of Dolle's. Before the invention of the pulling machine, small 8–10 pound batches of candy were pulled by hand on a hook attached to a wall.

Donnie Timmons (left) and Bunky Dolle share some laughs while forming salt water taffy to fit inside the Model K wrapping machine.

Bunky Dolle stirs freshly made caramel popcorn in the display case. The Dolle's building had rolling doors, as seen in the background. The doors were quite temperamental and were becoming an issue. They were very worn from use and the elements and often got stuck in their frames.

Katherine Roberg and Bunky Dolle are pictured behind the popcorn case making popcorn in large batches and prepackaging it. The popcorn boxes were packaged in the traditional cardboard boxes, then slipped inside a plastic bag. The bags were lined up in the display cases, ready for customers.

In 1972, Theo and Thomas Pachides are pictured in their apartment above Dolle's in Rehoboth Beach. Thomas immigrated to the United States from Greece in 1907, when he was 15 years old. A few years later, Theo immigrated from Greece as well. Even though they lived on the ocean and Thomas had a passion for fishing, Theo wanted nothing to do with the water. The ship she sailed on as a young girl from Greece was battered by wind and turbulent seas. The seasickness she endured on that voyage was enough to keep her out of and off of water for the remainder of her life. Her lifelong focus was clearly set on running her beloved candy store. Work was her hobby. Below is a photograph of the Pachideses with their three grandchildren, Carol Ibach, Thomas Ibach, and Signe Holmgren Murray. (Both, courtesy of Signe Holmgren Murray.)

Thomas Pachides and daughter Helen Pachides Holmgren are pictured working together. Helen and Constance "Connie" took the reins from their mother, Theo, as operators of Dolle's in Rehoboth Beach. They followed in Theo's footsteps, being dedicated and extremely hardworking women. Thomas Pachides continued to make all of the candies at Dolle's in Rehoboth Beach until he grew too old. Thomas and Carol Ibach's mother, Alexandra, did not work in the business. Rather, she raised her two children in Wilmington, Delaware. (Courtesy of Thomas Ibach.)

Pamela Winters, pictured with Bunky Dolle, was working at the Carousel Hotel in Ocean City and met a woman who came into the hotel with a pet monkey. Later on, she saw the same woman at the Bonfire restaurant. The lady was adamant about having her nephew meet Pamela. On May 4, 1974, Bunky Dolle and Pamela Winters met at a crab feast hosted by Bunky's aunt, Maxine English Kellem. Tweety the monkey was in attendance as well.

Maxine Kellem's matchmaking was a success, and in 1976, Bunky Dolle married Pamela Winters. Pictured is Bunky and his best man, Donnie Timmons.

Pictured behind manager Katherine Roberg is a glass case filled with fudge. At the time, Dolle's purchased fudge from NECCO. The candy stand simply did not have the space for making confections other than salt water taffy, mellow mints, caramels, and popcorn. Also pictured are the rolling cabinets and cases. To the left, people are standing in front of Thrasher's French Fries. This is one of the last photographs taken in the 1926 Dolle's.

On December 12, 1977, the Dolle's building that was constructed after the fire of 1925 was razed. Poor wiring and insurance issues led to its demise. In addition to the failing construction, the rolling doors, which were only locked with a pin, were not deemed secure. There was no choice but to tear the building down and start new. These photographs show the first stages of demolition.

The lot was cleared and cleaned rather quickly, and construction began on a new, more modern building that would take Dolle's into future decades. Seen in this photograph are the Cork Bar building, the second-floor apartments, and the Alaska Stand and Atlantic Hotel.

This photograph of the lot with steel beams jutting out from the sand shows the side of the Sportland arcade building. The new Dolle's was designed to have four bays in the front, two of which were to be used by Dolle's and the other two by tenants. It also included three apartments, all with views of the boardwalk and the ocean. The evolution of Dolle's of Ocean City included the purchase of a plot of land next to 9 Wicomico Street to use as a parking lot. The land was purchased from the Kohr family of Kohr Bros. Custard shops.

A few surprises turned up with the demolition of the old Dolle's building, including the popcorn box at left. Popcorn boxes were used as shims in the interiors of the walls when the building was constructed in 1926. Since the boxes were sealed within the walls, they remained in near perfect condition. Graphics from these rare boxes have been copied and used in current candy packaging at the Dolle's of Ocean City. Below, two figures, standing at about two and a half feet tall, were discovered behind a hot water heater. The figures were from the band organ off the original Dolle's merry-go-round. It is believed that they were removed from the property before the fire of 1925, which ensured their survival.

After construction was completed in the spring of 1978, Bunky and Pam Dolle held a grand opening. They invited guests to view old photographs and vintage boxes from the extensive history of Dolle's. Guest were also invited behind the scenes to see the new building, complete with a new air-conditioned chocolate shop that had a separate entrance from the bustling boardwalk. The outpouring of love from the community of Ocean City and the surrounding areas is shown in this small sample of cards saved from flower arrangements given on the grand opening. Helen and Connie from the Dolle's of Rehoboth Beach made salt water taffy for Dolle's to sell during its grand opening, easing the stress on Bunky and Pamela.

Mr. & Mrs. Rudolph W. Dolle, Jr.
cordially invite you to celebrate
the opening of the new

Dolle Building
Open House

Friday, April twenty-first
7 to 11 p.m.
Dolle Building
Wicomico St. at the Boardwalk
(opposite the pier)
Ocean City, Maryland

Please present
invitation at the door

During the grand opening, Bunky and Pam Dolle were not completely prepared for the business that would ensue that day. Here, Bunky struggles to serve customers as he tries to also welcome them as honored guests.

Bunky Dolle is seen in the new candy shop, referred to as the chocolate shop, which was complete with air-conditioning, display cases, and windows for customers to view the candy manufacturing. The interior shop meant a whole new world for candy at Dolle's. Now, Dolle's was capable of selling items that required a cool environment, including a full line of chocolates, gummy candies, and licorice.

With the shop windows behind him, Bunky Dolle adjusts the hooks on a newly purchased pulling machine. The manufacturing was to be seen by all, and new equipment was deemed necessary. Although the old equipment was obsolete, it has been kept as a reminder of the past.

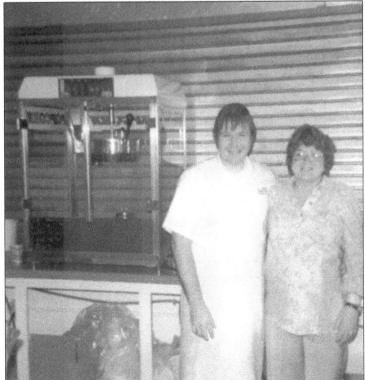

Bunky and Pamela Dolle were not only excited for their brand new building with new equipment and a new chocolate shop, they were excited for the next generation to enter into the world in November 1978. The year was looking very promising for the newlyweds.

Unfortunately, tragedy struck on July 20, 1978. In the height of the season, Bunky and Pam Dolle were working the candy counters as usual. Bunky went into the back hallway of Dolle's toward the office behind the Cork Bar only to find the back building completely engulfed in flames. The fire was devastating for the family. However, the Ocean City community banded together to help get Dolle's back up and running so it would not lose its summer business. Brasure's was credited with cleaning up quickly, and Dan Gladden took the helm managing the employees to get things back to normal. All of the candy on the scene had to be thrown out, and new candy had to be made. The Cork Bar had to throw out all liquor and beer that was not sealed. Because of the support of the community and the hard work of so many, both the Cork Bar and Dolle's were able to reopen their doors within four days—a true blessing for the seasonal businesses.

Resort Landmark Damaged In Fire

By TOM LEONARD
Of The Times Mail

OCEAN CITY – Dolle's, an Ocean City boardwalk landmark since 1910, was temporarily closed today after a fire, which began late Thursday destroyed three storerooms and an apartment at the rear of a complex of several stores.

Agency Dispute Decision Is Due

By ROWAN SCARBOROUGH
Of The Times Mail

The County Council is expected to announce a decision Aug. 1 on whether to allow the Commission on Aging to operate the SSI-funded senior citizen centers in Wicomico County.

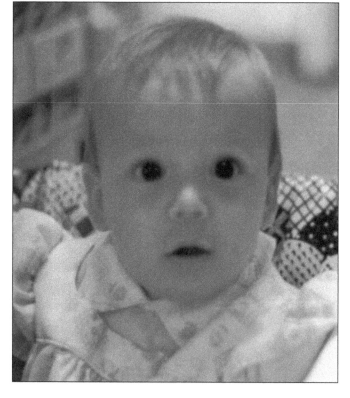

In September 1978, on the day of the baby shower being held for Pamela Dolle, Evelyn Dolle Dean Adams Gunby passed away at the age of 62. Her heath had been failing through the 1970s, so her day-to-day tasks had been taken over by Katherine Roberg, Donnie Timmons, and Bunky and Pam Dolle. On November 22, 1978, Anna Marie Dolle was born. The growing family lived in one of the apartments above Dolle's in the summers and at the family home in Bethany Beach during the off season. This photograph shows Anna rolling around in her walker on the sales floor of Dolle's. Boxes of stacked salt water taffy are seen behind her.

Eight

THE 1980s

Boardwalk — Ocean City, Maryland   Photo by R.C. Pulling

The 1980s proved to be a very good decade for the Dolle's of Ocean City. Visitors flocked to the boardwalk, and record-breaking sales were made. It was a decade of hard work, as Bunky and Pam Dolle grew the business while paying off the debts of the new building and new candy-making equipment. Donnie Timmons ended his partnership with Dolle's and went on to purchase Boardwalk Dairyland from Pete and Gladys Dumser. It was the beginning of the growth of Ocean City's most popular ice cream business, Dumser's Dairyland. At the same time businesses were growing and expanding on Wicomico Street, the Dolle's of Rehoboth Beach was undergoing its own changes.

Pam Dolle, wearing her Dolle's uniform, worked evenings through the summer. She managed the staff in addition to purchasing, scheduling, merchandising, and cleaning. All of this was done while learning a business completely new to her but second nature to her husband.

Bunky Dolle's heart, on the other hand, was truly in candy making. It simply was (and is) in his blood. With a penchant for all things confection, Bunky honed his candy-making skills by networking with other candy makers and attending candy-making schools throughout the country. The husband and wife made a great balanced team—one concentrated on the candy while the other focused on the business, much like their neighbors in Rehoboth Beach. Here, Bunky is making an old-fashioned candy called braided or plaited mints. Long pieces of mints were braided together in strands before they were left to "mellow" and become soft, with a melt-in-your-mouth consistency.

Katherine Roberg was a dependable manager at Dolle's for over 45 years. She adopted the Dolle family as her own and ran the shop as she saw fit. She was a link to the past, having been friends with the Dolle, English, and Dennis families.

In this photograph from 1980, taken on the north corner of the Dolle's in Ocean City, the square windows of the chocolate shop can be seen. Three sizes of popcorn boxes are on display on the caramel popcorn case, keeping with the consistency of branding and product.

With the growing popularity and availability of plastics, Dolle's was now able to offer caramel popcorn in airtight containers. Since the early 1980s, three sizes of plastic tubs have been available with popcorn being filled to order. In the past, decorative tin kitchen canisters in four sizes (typically used for sugar, coffee, tea, and flour) were used as caramel popcorn containers. The popcorn was scooped into the container and then a piece of paper was placed on top before the lid was secured. The paper between the product and the lid ensured a tight seal. The tin canisters were considered wasteful, as they would dent and rust, so plastic tubs were welcomed by Dolle's and its customers.

In 1981, employee photographs became a tradition with the Dolle's staff. In front of the large wooden sign on the northern brick wall of Dolle's, the Dolle family and staff smile for the camera after a busy summer season. Featured in this photograph are longtime employees, including Katherine Roberg (second row, fourth from left), her niece Elaine (first row, second from right), Anna Dolle (on Elaine's lap), and Pam and Bunky Dolle at far right.

Like in generations past, Anna Dolle enjoys some playtime on the boardwalk. At left is Mitch Lovell, son of Hugh and Donna Lovell, owners of Grace's jewelry shop. Grace's was next door to the Dolle's building and was known for its inventory of trendy jewelry. Mitch's grandparents were tenants of the apartments above the Dolle's Restaurant/Cork Bar building for many years.

The Dolle family opened several other locations in Ocean City, including this shop, opened in 1980 at 143rd Street, on the opposite end of town from the Wicomico Street location. Manufacturing was done at the boardwalk shop and products were transported here as needed.

On July 6, 1982, Bunky and Pam Dolle welcomed a son, Andrew Dolle, into the world. Having a baby in the middle of the summer season posed unique challenges for the family. However, Pam met the demands of the business and continued to do paperwork while in the hospital.

In 1982, the Dolle family closed the location at 143rd Street and opened a shop in the up-and-coming Ocean Plaza Mall at Ninety-fourth Street in Ocean City. The store, with an abundance of shelving in front and behind the counter, offered space for Dolle's to include a wide variety of plush toys and other gifts. It also gave the Dolles the opportunity to have a store open year-round. The Valentine's and Christmas holidays were decorated for and celebrated in this store. The shop closed its doors when the mall closed in 2002.

Pictured here is a view of Dolle's and the pier building in 1983. Long gone were the days of a ballroom and live music in the building. Instead, the Ripley's Believe It or Not! museum became the attraction there. The pier building included games in the walkway, which led to more amusements and rides out on the pier.

In 1984, Thomas Pachides passed away at the age of 93. His grandson Thomas Ibach moved from the Wilmington area to Rehoboth Beach to take his grandfather's place in the business. Ibach was no stranger to the business, as he had worked during the summers at Dolle's since he was 10 years old. His cousin Signe and his two aunts continued to be involved in running the business while Thomas focused his efforts on candy making. (Above, courtesy of Thomas Ibach; below, courtesy of Signe Holmgren-Murray.)

In 1985, the Dolle's of Ocean City celebrated its 75th anniversary and marked the special date with a commemorative salt water taffy box. A 75th anniversary seal was printed on a limited supply of boxes.

Anna and Andrew Dolle are pictured in 1986 in front of Dolle's with its roll-down steel doors. The doors have provided protection against storms, the elements, and crime, something that the simple rolling wooden and glass doors of old could not do. Anna and Andrew were accustomed to coming to Dolle's after school so that their parents could finish working.

The area behind the counter in 1988 was a clean and efficient workplace. Glass cases, custom built by the Charles Brown Glass Company, were the perfect new way to display candy. At left, built into the counter, is the hot pad used to seal cellophane wrapping on boxes of taffy.

In 1988, Bunky Dolle hand dips individual pieces of salt water taffy in dark chocolate. After attending candy school in California that year, he returned with a knowledge of chocolate making. Here, he uses another new piece of equipment that wrapped and sealed each salt water taffy box in cellophane. Long gone were the days when employees had to wrap each one by hand.

Bunky Dolle always enjoyed the physical labor of making candy. With a large wooden paddle, he stirs a batch of caramel popcorn in a copper kettle. The caramel is made using a mixture of brown sugar, white sugar, corn syrup, butter, air popped popcorn, and salt—all added in at precise moments to ensure a specific taste. The Dolle's of Ocean City and the Dolle's of Rehoboth Beach use two different recipes for their popcorn. The biggest flavor difference is the addition of molasses in the caramel popcorn in Rehoboth Beach.

With the increase in manufacturing in the 1980s, Rudolph Dolle purchased a corn syrup tank to store the mass quantities of syrup needed. Syrup is pumped directly from this tank into the kitchens. Corn syrup was and still is delivered via a tanker truck at 25,000 pounds per delivery.

This picture of the front of Dolle's of Ocean City in 1989 shows the new, large, refrigerated, rounded-glass cases. These cases increased the types of candy that were able to be sold in the open stand to include chocolates and other candies that were subject to melting.

Signe Holmgren Murray photographed her mother and aunt working diligently at Dolle's in Rehoboth Beach. Cotton candy hangs from displays, and stacks of boxed taffy are on the counter in preparation for a busy day. (Courtesy of Signe Holmgren Murray.)

Nine

THE 1990S

The 1990s was another decade of change and growth for both the Dolle's of Ocean City and the Dolle's of Rehoboth Beach. Anna and Andrew Dolle, grandchildren of Rudolph and Elaine Dolle, both began working in the shops, while Thomas Ibach was setting up a new shop of his own in Rehoboth Beach. The 1990s were also a time when technology was finding its way into the business, giving Dolle's new ways to make and sell candy.

Bunky Dolle began molding chocolate in the mid-1980s. The majority of his handmade creations were made for Easter and included a wide variety of chocolate bunnies. Here, Bunky makes one of his chocolate creations in the candy room behind the chocolate shop on the boardwalk. Behind him, the original taffy hook that his grandfather and father used to pull salt water taffy by hand is attached to the wall. The automated, four-hook salt water taffy puller (below) took the place of this hook in the early days of Dolle's.

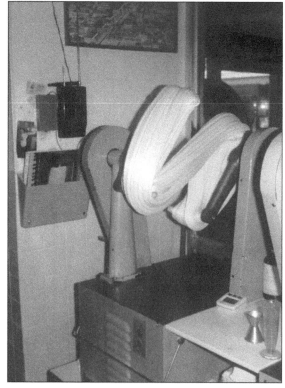

In 1991, Thomas Ibach recognized that the Rehoboth Beach area lacked a quality chocolate business. He opened Ibach's By the Sea, a chocolate and candy shop just steps from the Dolle's of Rehoboth Beach. The air-conditioned shop offered a full selection of homemade chocolates made by Ibach. He turned the apartments above Dolle's into a chocolate factory, where he continues to make all of the candies for the chocolate store. Selections of chocolates expanded into the holiday markets, with items such as hand-molded Easter bunnies, hand-rolled Easter eggs, and Christmas candies.

In 1993, Pamela Dolle stands at the corner of Dolle's with a birthday cake in her arms. Anna Dolle is seen to the left of Pam, in front of the popcorn case. The cake was for the celebration of Bunky's birthday, which the Dolle family as well as the Dolle's employees enjoyed together.

Wilbur "Bill" Winters, Pamela Dolle's father, stands outside the hallway behind Dolle's. Bill joined the team at Dolle's in 1986 as a taffy machine operator. He and his wife retired to Ocean City from Silver Springs, Maryland, and Bill enjoyed his post retirement job at Dolle's. Katherine Roberg is also pictured in this photograph from 1994.

In 1995, Thomas Ibach began his official ownership of Dolle's Candyland of Rehoboth Beach. After working for the company for years during the summer and learning candy making from his grandfather and Bunky Dolle, it was a natural fit for him to continue the business. In 1998, Thomas Ibach welcomed triplets into his family.

In 1997, Bunky Dolle stands on the same corner of Wicomico Street and the boardwalk where his relatives have been photographed for decades. Bunky and Pam's children were in college and high school at the time. Since age 12, each child has worked every summer in the candy stand, following in the footsteps of their ancestors.

Ten

BIG STEPS IN THE 2000S

The 2000s was an extremely busy period of growth for the Dolle family. In May 2000, Anna Dolle graduated from American University, and Andrew Dolle graduated from high school. Andrew continued his education locally so that he could work with Anna at Dolle's. They began to focus on Dolle's as a career, seriously developing and executing plans to grow the company, all with the consultation of their experienced parents.

Makers of
Ocean City's
Original
Salt Water Taffy
Since 1910

Please Join Us In The Celebration of Dolle's
"Grand Re-Opening" & Ribbon Cutting

Place: Dolle's Candyland 500 S. Boardwalk
& Wicomico Street
Ocean City, MD
Date: Wednesday April 21, 2004
Time: 4:30~8:30 p.m
R.S.V.P: (410)289-6000
Looking forward to seeing you there!

During the winter of 2003, Anna and Andrew Dolle redesigned the candy shop as well as the manufacturing kitchens. All of the candy machinery, including pulling machines, cut and wrap machines, and packaging machinery, were moved to an updated facility at 9 Wicomico Street, the same building that once housed the public restrooms/apartments/Mr. Donut/flower shop decades ago. A kitchen, complete with a boiler and large vacuum cookers, was added onto the back of the building. In addition, the small 300-square-foot chocolate shop was torn down to make room for a 1,200-square-foot store, all on the footprint of the old manufacturing area.

Lisa Williams Hyatt is seen processing mail orders. Still a large part of the Dolle's business, customers enjoy sending Dolle's candies worldwide. Gone are the days of simple paper receipts. With technology and the use of the internet, customers can simply go online to place orders for products manufactured and shipped from where it all began, on Wicomico Street and the boardwalk in Ocean City.

A major change in the facade was created with the construction of a north entrance. The northern foyer of the shop is where the candy stoves once stood. At the grand reopening in April 2004, town and state dignitaries came to a ribbon cutting for the "new" shop. The grand reopening marked the beginning of the passing of the business to the next generation, Anna Dolle Bushnell and Andrew Dolle. Pictured above are, from left to right, Raymond Chandler, Paul Rouchard, Mary Dean Thompson Rouchard, Pamela Dolle, Anna Dolle Bushnell, Andrew Dolle, Sen. Jim Mathias, and Bunky Dolle.

Sean Blanchard operates the salt water taffy machinery purchased by Rudolph Dolle in 1953. Shortly after Rudolph purchased the Forgrove cut and wrap machine, he bought the other two machines seen here. One is the batch former, which, with four rollers, rolls large masses of taffy into a graded piece that is later fed into the rope sizer machine. The rope sizer forms the taffy into a rope with gradient sized wheels that force the candy through. The candy is formed into just the right diameter to fit into the cut and wrap machine. This photograph was taken in the building at 9 Wicomico Street.

In 2006, another location was opened, this one at 120th Street in Ocean City.

In 2007, the building that sat directly behind Dolle's, which housed Dolle's Restaurant and then the Cork Bar with the sub shop on the eastern corner, was torn down. Issues with the structure's integrity forced Dolle's to demolish it and rebuild. The building was constructed according to the specifications of the Cork Bar's owners so that they could continue their business in the atmosphere their customers grew to love. The second story of the building was replaced with more manufacturing space for Dolle's. Upstairs, a fudge and caramel kitchen was created in addition to a packaging plant and storage areas.

By 2008, Andrew Dolle and Anna Dolle Bushnell had both started their own families. Like their relatives, their children have grown up in the business. The children have followed in their ancestors' footsteps, all having their first jobs in candy packaging. From left to right are (first row) Anna Dolle Bushnell with Hailey and Brady Bushnell; (second row) Bunky Dolle, Pam Dolle, Andrew Dolle, and Andrea Nagy Dolle.

Here, employees pose for the staff photograph in 2009. In comparison to the staff photographs of the 1980s, the number of staff at Dolle's has more than doubled. Candy is not only manufactured for Dolle's, but is made for the wholesale trade as well.

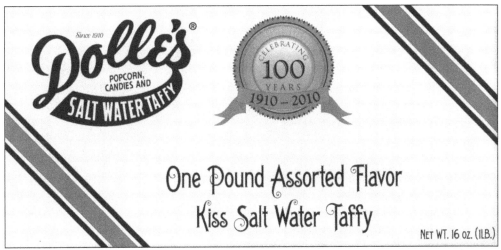

Dolle's Candyland of Ocean City celebrated its 100th year in 2010. A commemorative salt water taffy box was made, highlighting the anniversary year. Events throughout the year-long celebration included promotional days when candy was priced at different "decade" pricing, giveaways for customers who brought old photos of Dolle's in, and a homecoming party for employees and longtime customers.

Around this time, Dolle's Candyland of Rehoboth Beach created a new design for its salt water taffy boxes. Still incorporating the Cape Henlopen Lighthouse, it also includes attractive illustrations not only of the beach and the Dolle's building, but also its salt water taffy.

In 2013, Anna Dolle Bushnell and Andrew Dolle opened a third location at Sixty-Seventh Street in Ocean City. Dolle's had never had a midtown location in Ocean City, but with the growing number of visitors, it has been successful.

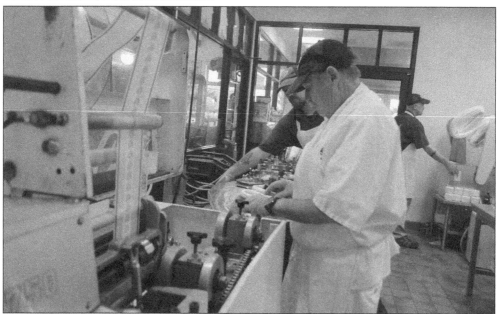

Rudolph Dolle is pictured making taffy with his son Andrew Dolle (right). The machinery seen here was purchased in 1983 and cuts and wraps the small square pieces of salt water taffy. The machinery was relocated to the Dolle's shop at Sixty-Seventh Street. Here, windows were built in to resemble the glass windows of the Dolle's candy stands from the 1920s. Customers can view candy being made at the shop, an old-fashioned sight enjoyed by many.

In the spring of 2018, Andrew Dolle and Anna Dolle Bushnell opened another Dolle's Candyland in West Ocean City, Maryland. Located within a mile and a half of the original Dolle's, the new location boasts a large shop with a small chocolate manufacturing area that can be seen by customers.

Andrew Dolle continues his family traditions and enjoys making candy on machinery passed down from generation to generation, like this Model K machine. In addition to the antique machinery, more computerized equipment like high tech printers, scales, and bagging machines have been purchased by the new generation.

Thomas Ibach still continues his family's legacy on the corner of the boardwalk and Rehoboth Avenue in Rehoboth Beach. His business has expanded to include his own brand, with the Ibach name proudly paired with Dolle's Candyland.

Dolle's of Ocean City at the corner of Wicomico Street and the boardwalk and Dolle's of Rehoboth Beach still stand proudly to this day. The tradition of the most perfect souvenirs, all timeless sweets made at the beach, still continues on the very corners where they began. (Above, courtesy of Robert Banach.)

Visit us at
arcadiapublishing.com